Festivals

Holi

by Rebecca Pettiford

Ideas for Parents and Teachers

Bullfrog Books let children practice reading informational text at the earliest reading levels. Repetition, familiar words, and photo labels support early readers.

Before Reading

- Discuss the cover photo. What does it tell them?

- Look at the picture glossary together. Read and discuss the words.

Read the Book

- "Walk" through the book and look at the photos. Let the child ask questions. Point out the photo labels.

- Read the book to the child, or have him or her read independently.

After Reading

- Prompt the child to think more. Ask: Have you ever celebrated Holi? What sorts of things do you see during this festival?

Bullfrog Books are published by Jump!
5357 Penn Avenue South
Minneapolis, MN 55419
www.jumplibrary.com

Library of Congress Cataloging-in-Publication Data

Names: Pettiford, Rebecca, author.
Title: Holi / by Rebecca Pettiford.
Description: Minneapolis, MN: Jump!, Inc., [2017]
Series: Festivals | Includes index.
Audience: Ages 5-8. | Audience: K to grade 3.
Identifiers: LCCN 2016023696 (print)
LCCN 2016031869 (ebook)
ISBN 9781620315323 (hard cover: alk. paper)
ISBN 9781620315866 (paperback)
ISBN 9781624964862 (e-book)
Subjects: LCSH: Holi (Hindu festival)—Juvenile literature. | Hinduism—Customs and practices—Juvenile literature. | Fasts and feasts—Hinduism—Juvenile literature. | India—Social life and customs—Juvenile literature. | CYAC: Holidays.
Classification: LCC BL1239.82.H65 P48 2017 (print)
LCC BL1239.82.H65 (ebook) | DDC 294.5/36—dc23
LC record available at https://lccn.loc.gov/2016023696

Editor: Kirsten Chang
Book Designer: Leah Sanders
Photo Researcher: Leah Sanders

Photo Credits: Age Fotostock, 10–11, 23br; Alamy, 8, 18–19, 22; Getty, 3, 6–7, 9, 12–13, 15, 20–21, 23tl, 23tr; iStock, 5; Karves/Shutterstock.com, 14–15; Shutterstock, cover, 1, 4, 16, 17, 19, 23ml, 23bl, 23mr, 24.

Printed in the United States of America at Corporate Graphics in North Mankato, Minnesota.

Table of Contents

Festival of Colors

It is spring in India.

It is time for Holi!

Holi is a Hindu festival.

It begins when
the moon is full.

It lasts for two days.

We make a big fire.

We remember a special boy.

His bad aunt Holika put him in a fire.

But he lived!

Holika

9

We celebrate good winning over evil.

How?

We get powder.

It comes in many colors.

We throw it
at each other.

We look like
rainbows.

Raj has a water gun.

He sprays us with color.

Look! Our dog is pink!

15

Watch out!

Dev has water balloons.

Too late!

Brij gets hit.

We eat gujiyas.
Yum!
They are sweet.

gujiyas

19

We sing.

We dance.

Holi is fun!

Colors of Holi

yellow
Yellow stands
for healing.

green
Green stands for
new beginnings.

red
Red stands for
love and beauty.

blue
Blue stands for
power and life.

pink
Pink stands
for joy.

Picture Glossary

festival
A special time when people gather to celebrate something.

Holika
An evil spirit in the Hindu religion who threw her nephew into a fire.

gujiyas
Indian sweets filled with dried fruit and coconut.

India
A country in South Asia.

Hindu
A person who follows the Hindu religion. Hindus believe in many gods.

powder
Any solid material that is crushed into dry, loose bits.

Index

To Learn More

Learning more is as easy as 1, 2, 3.

1) Go to www.factsurfer.com

2) Enter "Holi" into the search box.

3) Click the "Surf" button to see a list of websites.

With factsurfer.com, finding more information is just a click away.